NEW METHODS
IN NEEDLEPOINT

HOPE HANLEY

NEW METHODS
IN NEEDLEPOINT

NEW YORK · CHARLES SCRIBNER'S SONS

Printed in the United States of America
SBN 684-10224-2
Library of Congress Catalog Card Number 66-20459

CREDITS

Pieces on pp. 37 and 70 worked by Lee Hanley and on p. 57 worked by Toby Hanley were finished by the author. The pillow on p. 55 was worked by Mrs. Katherine M. Frease and the tote bag on p. 69 designed and worked by Mrs. Helen Grover; all others by the author.

TABLE OF CONTENTS

6

With the exception of footstools, chair seats and pillows, most needlepoint projects are unmountable at home. The average needlepointer is loath to try to "finish" her own work for fear of botching the fruit of many hours' work. This book will show how with one basic stitch more useful articles can be completed at home. The following method of finishing lends itself to projects with a less formal air, and the materials used to make them may be less formal. For the most part the projects included in this book are "quick and easy" to complete, and can be made of less expensive materials, and since they are not designed as heirlooms it is practical to choose more currently fashionable colors. The old stand-by colors may take a rest while the more frivolous ones have their day. Perhaps you will choose to make some cushions to use with your present slipcovers, or maybe a glasses case to match your everyday pocketbook, or an envelope purse to go with your new coat.

Some of the projects will be suitable only for the experienced needlepoint engineer, others could serve nicely for Girl Scout merit badge projects. Three of the pieces used in the illustrations were made by the author's children, aged nine and ten at the time. This basic finishing stitch is an imaginative one, please use it so. Perhaps the instructions given here will spark you into some inventions of your own. Everything has not been done in needlepoint yet!

ACKNOWLEDGMENTS

The author would like to offer sincere thanks to Miss Doris Bowman of the Smithsonian Institution, and to Mr. James M. O'Neill of the District of Columbia Public Library for their usual cheerful assistance. My thanks to Mr. Louis J. Gartner, Crafts Editor of the *House & Garden* magazine for his helpful suggestions and encouragement. To Mrs. Katherine Morrison Frease and Mrs. Helen Grover goes the author's praise for their industry and skill in completing projects to illustrate this book. To Miss Elinor Parker, my heartfelt gratitude for the continued benefits of her good taste and judgement.

My acknowledgments to the booklet, *Stitched Rugs and Tapestries,* edited by Patience Horne, Middlesex, England, and to S. I. Matthew's essay on needle-made rugs in the *Handbook of Crafts,* edited by Griselda Lewis, for introducing me to the binding stitch or the plaited edge stitch.

NEW METHODS
IN NEEDLEPOINT

CHAPTER ONE

MATERIALS

CANVAS

Needlepoint canvas comes in two varieties, single thread and double thread. The single thread is known as mono-canvas, uni-canvas and "uni". It ranges in mesh size from the finest gauze to eight mesh to the inch. It is usually white though it can be bought in ecru.

Double thread canvas is called penelope. Penelope is usually ecru and most stores carry it only in ten mesh to the inch. It is made also in twelve and fourteen mesh to the inch but this is not readily available. The distinctive feature of penelope is that the double warp threads are woven closer together than the double woof threads.

Rug canvas also has double threads but they are evenly spaced from each other. The most available sizes of rug canvas are four or five mesh to the inch. It can be obtained in as low a mesh as three to the inch. Latchet rug hooking is done on rug canvas, so any store that has rug hooking supplies will carry it as well as a needlepoint shop. The rug canvas that works the best with rug wool and bulky wool is called "Smyrna" rug canvas. It comes in various meshes but you should specify five mesh. Rug canvas is usually white or yellow and comes in thirty-six to forty inch widths.

The better quality canvases of all kinds have highly polished threads. Buy only flawless canvas, knots and weak-looking threads may come apart if much stretching is required when blocking and finishing your work. Always work the canvas with the selvedge on the side.

A spool of carpet thread in white is necessary for the preparation of the canvas on some of the projects. Any notions counter will have it.

WOOL

Proper needlepoint wools are crewel wool, Persian wool, tapestry wool and rug wool. Crewel wool comes in a great variety of colors and can be bought anywhere that crewel or needlepoint supplies are sold. It fits very nicely on sixteen mesh canvas and other fine mesh canvas. Persian wool also comes in a wide range of colors but it can be bought only in needlepoint shops. It is a three thread strand, which can often be bought by the strand, a most economical arrangement. It can be used all three threads at once on ten mesh canvas or one thread at a time on canvas as fine as sixteen mesh. Tapestry wool comes in a limited range of colors and is available in department stores. A few needlepoint shops carry a wider range of colors in an imported tapestry wool. Tapestry wool fits ten mesh mono-canvas and penelope.

Rug wool is available in a good range of colors at needlepoint shops. It is sold by the pound or half pound. There are two different sizes of rug wool so make sure you are buying the right size for your canvas. One wool is so thick it is used on three mesh to the inch canvas, the other wool is lighter. The wool sold for rug hooking unfortunately is too fine for our use. Almost all wools now are mothproof.

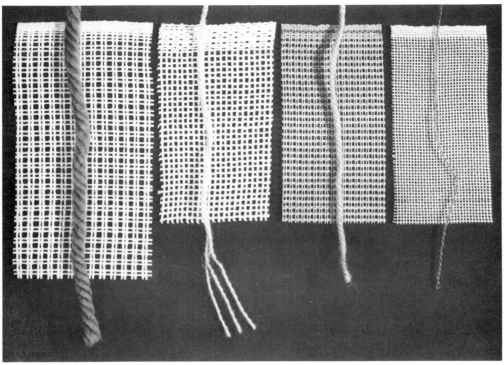

LEFT TO RIGHT. 5 mesh rug canvas with rug wool
10 mesh mono-canvas with Persian wool spread to show
three strands
10 mesh penelope with tapestry wool
18 mesh canvas with crewel wool, mono-canvas

Any wool is fair game for needlepoint *if* it covers the canvas properly and if you don't care if the finished item does not wear forever. Real needlepoint wool has a long smooth fibre while knitting wool has a shorter wiry fibre. Because of this some knitting wool will ball while being worked and afterwards under heavy use. Other wools thin out as they are drawn repeatedly through the canvas so that short strands are recommended.

13

Now you know the disadvantages. The advantages of using knitting wool are its availability and its economy. Bernat's nylo-sport yarn is considerably less expensive than Persian wool, worsted is cheaper and brighter than tapestry wool, and bulky wool such as Columbia-Minerva's Contempo or Bernat's Shaker-spun is much cheaper and lighter in weight than rug wool. The wool used for rya rugs though less even in texture than other wools might find a use in needlepoint. Experiment with the materials you have at hand. The essential criterion is: does the wool cover the canvas?

The regular half cross stitch is recommended for plain areas of your work on double thread canvas, rather than the basket weave or continental stitch, because it makes less bulk in the back of the canvas. Of course, on mono-canvas you will have to use the basket weave because half cross does not work satisfactorily.

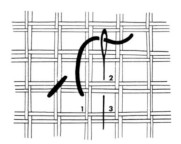

The Half Cross Stitch

NEEDLES

Needlepoint needles are sold under the name of tapestry or embroidery needles. The higher the number on the package label, the higher mesh on which it can be used. The lower the number, the larger the mesh can be. Size 17 tapestry needles will do well for ten to fourteen mesh per inch canvas, size 19 will do for sixteen to eighteen mesh per inch and there are two sizes of needle that can be used on rug canvas. All needles should have a long eye and a blunt point, the finer needles will be sharper than the large ones. Things to consider when choosing the right needle are: does the needle slide through the canvas easily? A badly fitting needle spreads the mesh of the canvas. Is it relatively easy to thread the needle? You don't want to split the wool too much dragging it through the eye.

BLOCKING

There is no need to send your finished work out to be blocked, it is simple to do at home. All you need is a flat wooden surface large enough to take your canvas and a box of aluminum tacks and a tack hammer. The wooden surface should be something on which you won't mind a few tack holes. The tacks must be aluminum, the other kind will rust. Tack some brown paper over the board and mark in crayon a general outline of the shape you want the canvas to be. Wet the canvas thoroughly and gently tug and pull it true again. Spread it out on the board and start tacking it about a half inch from the finished work, first top and bottom, then side and side, quartering it and re-quartering it until there is a tack about every inch all the way around the canvas. Rug canvas will need tacks about every two or three inches. You will have to stretch and tug as you tack. It will take about twenty-four hours for the canvas to dry. Gently remove the tacks.

If the canvas is just a little bit pulled out of shape when you finish working it, you may be able to get away with just pressing it with a damp cloth and a hot iron then tugging it true again, and blocking will not be necessary.

15

CHAPTER TWO

THE BINDING STITCH

The basic stitch about to be described is known as the binding stitch or the plaited edge stitch. Its original use was to cover the selvedge of strip needlepoint rugs. In this book we will use it as an edger and we will also use it to bind pieces of canvas together to finish them. Used as a way to fasten canvas together the stitch is fairly hard-wearing as the wool is passed through each mesh twice. It is a decorative stitch, the slightly bulky braid fitting proportionately on fine canvas as well as rug canvas. The binding stitch can also be used in place of masking tape around the edges of raw canvas to keep it from ravelling as it is worked.

The binding stitch can be used to turn corners on single thicknesses of canvas and can be used to box corners. The stitch is done over the folded edge of the canvas. It works best on two thread canvas. It will work on mono-canvas if you treat it as a two thread canvas. Thus, where directions say to fold, just fold so that two lines of canvas are involved instead of one, then work the binding stitch over the two threads.

Do a practice strip before you try the binding stitch on your finished work. If you are using a two thread canvas fold a scrap of it along one set of warp or woof threads. If you are using mono-canvas, fold along two threads of canvas as stated above.

Several of the projects in this book require that a hem of canvas about four mesh deep be turned back before the needlepoint is worked. This is the customary way to do the ends of strip rugs. The needlepoint stitches are then worked to the edge of the fold of the canvas. They are worked right through both thicknesses of canvas just as if it were one piece of canvas, the mesh matched exactly, one on top of the other.

The canvas will be a little thicker than before but a lot less than one would expect. The hem will not pull out since the wool is holding it firmly in place. On some other projects you can fold the canvas hem back after you have completed the needlepoint and are ready to do the binding stitch and then you will not have to work through the two thicknesses of canvas. Just fold the canvas on the line of mesh next to your finished work.

To do the binding stitch, hold the canvas with the wrong side facing you. Fasten the end of the wool in the backs of nearby stitches. You will be working from left to right. With the needle pointed toward you, work two stitches over the fold in the

Folded canvas, tacked down with carpet thread

17

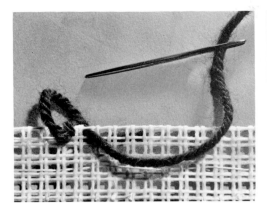 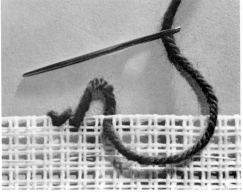

Folded canvas with first two stitches worked on it

Needle having been thrust through hole four

canvas using up two holes. These stitches will form the base of the stitch only and will not be repeated again. Come through the second hole again.

With the wool coming from your side of the canvas skip one hole of mesh and go over the edge and into the back of the fourth hole. With the wool still coming from your side of the canvas go over the edge again and into the back of the second hole. (Yes, one of your beginning stitches is already there.)

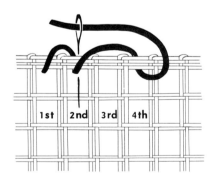

The Binding Stitch

Needle having been thrust through hole two again

Needle back up to hole five

Go over the edge again and into the back of the fifth hole, over the edge again and into the back of the third hole. Continue this back and forth stitch on up the edge of the canvas. Remember to always bring the wool over the edge of the canvas and always go in the back of the canvas.

To fasten off an old piece of wool and begin a new one you must pay close attention to the current direction of the stitch. Bring the wool through to the wrong side of the canvas and fasten it into the backs of nearby stitches. Fasten in the new thread close by and pick up the direction in which you were going before. You want it to appear from the right side as if the new thread were coming out of the hole that the old thread went in.

To finish the stitch, choose the stitch hole at which you want to stop and work right up to it, going back and forth right up to the final hole. If you are meeting the beginning of your work when doing a circular piece, work over the beginning two stitches as if they were not there and then stop. If you are working the edging before the side seams are sewn, leave hanging a tag of wool six inches long to use later to work over the seam.

Mono-canvas with Binding Stitch, showing
the two mesh

Two pieces of canvas being joined by
Binding Stitch

To sew two pieces of canvas together with the binding stitch you must have the same number of mesh on the fold of each piece. You will be matching the canvas mesh for mesh and each side must equal the other. Hold the two pieces together with the wrong sides facing each other. Work the binding stitch over both edges as if they were one edge, matching the mesh exactly. To start and finish a thread work it up into the backs of nearby stitches as before with a single thickness, only come up between the two pieces. The basic principle of using the binding stitch as a joiner is that for every mesh there must be a matching mesh. This principle applies even to turning corners.

The following projects progress by degree of difficulty. It is suggested that one of the first three projects be tried before you tackle any of the more intricate ones. Each one will show you a new way of handling the binding stitch.

CHAPTER THREE

A WASTE BASKET COVER

The first thing to do in making a waste basket is to buy the waste basket. You will need a straight-sided metal basket, it can be any shape, round, oval or square. It must have the same circumference at the top as at the bottom. If you plan to cover a letter box to match, or a pencil holder, the requirement is the same: straight sides. Rug canvas will work up the quickest for the waste basket, ten mesh penelope will do for the letter box or pencil holder.

Measure the circumference of the basket and then add a half inch for the amount of canvas that will be drawn up as the canvas is worked. (One-quarter inch for the letter box or pencil holder.) Measure the basket from top to bottom and add another half inch to your calculations to compensate for the loss in width that will result when you are stretching the canvas at completion. (One-quarter inch again for the box or holder.) It is better to have the cover a little too big from top to bottom than too small. Outline in pencil on the canvas the area to be worked. Then add a couple of inches on the short ends for the seam allowance. Add four mesh top and bottom for the fold-back hem. Check to make sure your calculations are correct before cutting the canvas.

Fold the canvas back at both top and bottom along the row of mesh that will have the edging on it later. (If you are using

mono-canvas fold along two threads of mesh.) Loosely baste the fold-back to the body of the canvas so that the meshes match up. Bind the short ends of the canvas with binding tape or masking tape so that the ends will not ravel as you work.

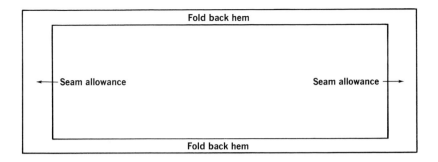

Fold back hem

Seam allowance ← ... → Seam allowance

Fold back hem

Now you are ready to design your cover. Remembering that the edging row of mesh will not count in your design, count off the mesh both warp and woof. Count the same number of squares off

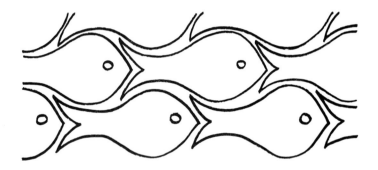

Sketched Out

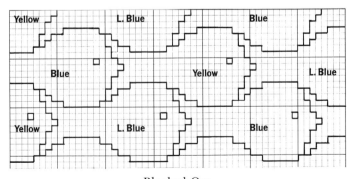

Yellow   L. Blue   Blue

Blue   Yellow   L. Blue

Yellow   L. Blue   Blue

Blocked Out

23

on graph paper and go to work. If you have never designed before, the best plan is to draw on the graph paper as if it were plain paper and then block out the pattern square by square.

Work your design and background, working right through the fold-back as if it were not there. When you have finished the work you may find that the canvas is only slightly pulled out of shape. You may be able to get away with just pressing it with a very damp cloth and a very hot iron, easing and stretching it true again. More likely, however, the canvas will be stretched quite out of shape. Wet it thoroughly and then stretch it true again, pulling first on one side and then the other. Tack it with aluminum tacks (to avoid rust) tautly on an old door or drawing board or what have you. You will have to tack it right through the body of the work on the long sides so tack sparingly.

When the canvas is dry and the tacks carefully removed, wrap the canvas around the waste basket for a final fitting before you sew up the side seam. If the canvas is too long to fit, snip out a row or so of stitches; if it is too short, add a few rows. If the canvas is too tall for the waste basket, which is not very likely, wet the canvas again and pull firmly on each end. This will make it longer length-wise but also shorter width-wise. When you are satisfied with the fit, sew the short sides together either by hand or by machine, working on the last worked row of needlepoint. If you prefer, you can join the ends by working a row of half cross stitches up the seam. To do this fold the canvas back along the last row of mesh next to the finished work. Hold the two folds together and work the half cross stitch up the mesh thus presented. Do this first with carpet thread and then with the wool.

Work the binding stitch around the top and bottom edges of the cover, starting at the seam and working from left to right. When you meet the beginning again try to work into the first two

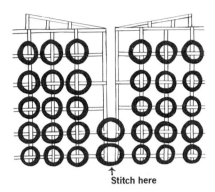

Stitch here

stitches so that the edging will look continuous. Trim the canvas on the inside of the fold-back on the seam allowance to reduce bulk at the seam. Trim the seam allowance canvas to within three mesh of the seam. Slip the cover on the basket and glue it in place with vinyl glue used very sparingly. The cover may be cleaned with one of the spray dry cleaners.

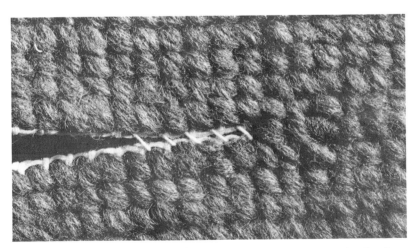

Two pieces of canvas joined at seam by row of stitches covering basting stitches

25

CHAPTER FOUR

THE FINE MESH GLASSES CASE

This glasses case should be made on fine mesh canvas, fourteen or sixteen mesh mono-canvas or ten mesh or less penelope canvas. Mark off on the canvas in pencil a square six inches by six inches and one-quarter. Measure a border of about one inch and a half on both six and one-quarter ends and mark them on the canvas. A border of four or five mesh should be drawn on the six inch ends. Cut the canvas around these boundaries.

Fold back the four or five mesh sides, fold on one set of

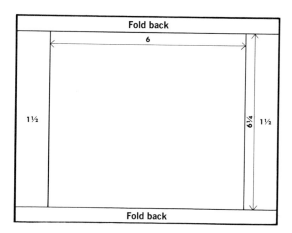

The Fine Mesh Glasses Case, worked on 18 mesh to the inch mono-canvas

mesh threads if you are using penelope and on two threads if mono-canvas. Baste the fold backs to the body of the canvas with carpet thread. Cover the other ends of the canvas with masking tape or binding tape, including the fold-back under the tape. This is to prevent any raveling of the canvas as you work.

Count off the mesh in both directions and then count the same number off on graph paper and design your case. The case pictured was worked in the half cross stitch and the triple leviathan stitch.

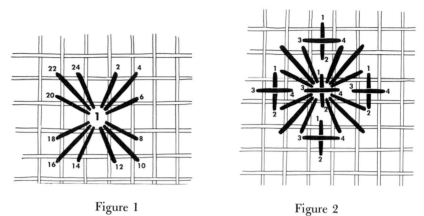

Figure 1   Figure 2

The Triple Leviathan Stitch

As you work the case, stitch through the fold-backs, matching up the mesh, and leaving the row of mesh bare on the fold-back edge on which you will do the binding stitch later. You may pull out the basting thread on the fold-back as you work. When

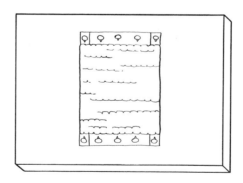

A stretched canvas

the needlepoint is finished and if it is just slightly out of shape, press it with a very damp cloth over it and then ease it gently back into shape. If it is very much out of shape you will have to wet the whole thing and then stretch it true again. Tack it with aluminum tacks to an old drawing board or clean plank covered with brown paper. Try to put very few tacks through the needle-point, if possible just use the bare canvas border.

The stretched canvas should dry in about twenty-four hours. Remove it from the board and sew the longer sides together by hand or machine along the last row of needlepoint on each side. Snip the excess canvas out of the inside fold-back to reduce bulk. Trim the border canvas to within four mesh of the seam. Work the binding stitch around the mouth of the case, starting at the seam and working around to the beginning again and over the first two stitches to give it a continuous look.

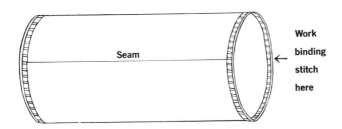

To close the bottom of the case, press the sides together and match up the mesh. Then, starting from the left, work the binding stitch right through both layers of mesh as if you were working just one layer. Start the stitch with only one beginning stitch and that one over the corner-most mesh. Then go ahead with the back and forth part of the stitch over the first set of matching mesh. Continue matching mesh for mesh to the other end and finish off by running the wool back and underneath the

29

Closing mouth of glasses case, showing corner. (This case worked in 10 mesh penelope)

stitches you have worked. If by chance the corners poke through bare, over-stitch one or two times.

Give the case a good steam blocking. Measure the case for the lining. Using the selvedge of the lining material at the mouth of the case cuts down bulk considerably. Sew the L-shaped seam of the lining and insert the lining into the case. Stitch the lining into place just under the binding stitch with matching thread.

Lining for glasses case

CHAPTER FIVE

THE RUG CANVAS
GLASSES CASE

Rug canvas is the only canvas to use for this case. For wool use rug wool or bulky knitting wool, preferably the latter because it is softer. The case makes up for its inflexibility of materials by its speed of construction. Not only that, it lines itself. On the other hand, it can only be made in stripes or solids because the stitch used, an adaptation of the oblique slav stitch done diagonally, does not lend itself readily to design work. Instead of going up two rows of mesh and over four rows as one is supposed to do, here

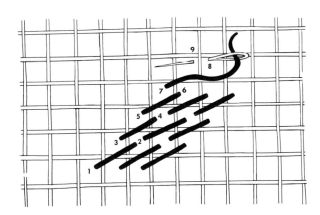

Adaptation of the Oblique Slav Stitch done diagonally

31

one goes up one row of mesh and over two. Once you catch on to the rhythm of it the stitch is sheer idiots' delight.

Measure a piece of rug canvas (try to use the five mesh) with a working area of six and one-quarter inches by six inches. Allow for a four mesh fold-back. In each corner gently snip out a four mesh square.

Fold back your fold-back on the fifth row of mesh on all four sides.

With carpet thread and needle ready, match up the mesh in the corners so that you can easily see through all three layers of canvas. Make a few basting stitches through the three layers of canvas to hold them in place and then lash the cut edge of the canvas to the folded edge. Baste your way to the next corner and do

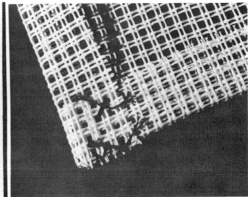

The four mesh square snipped out   The corner folded, basted and lashed

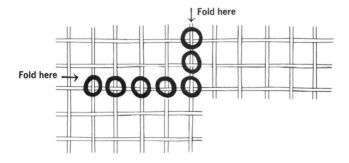

the same lashing of edges, go on around the rest of the canvas in this way. The basting threads may be left in as you work or may be removed, but the lashing threads should be left in until just before you work the binding stitch over them, then you should delicately snip them out.

Still armed with your carpet thread and needle, hold the slightly longer edges, the six and one-quarter edges of your little piece of canvas together. Matching up the mesh, sew them together with an over and over stitch to form a little roll of canvas. Sewing these edge mesh together will give you thirty rows of mesh around, if you used five mesh canvas.

33

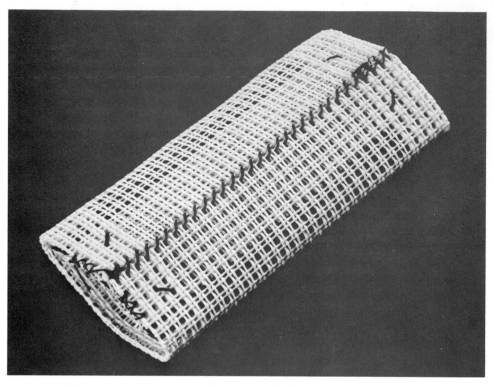

The glasses case canvas ready to be worked, showing the over and over stitched seam

The case pictured has two rows of yellow followed by one row of blue, or a set of three rows repeated ten times. Count the number of mesh on your roll and figure out your stripes. You must use one piece of wool for each stripe, so use a piece of wool about two feet long for your first row. Measure what is left of that first two-foot piece and subtract from twenty-four inches. The result will be how much wool you will need for each row.

Work the oblique slav stitch done diagonally, as diagrammed above, from one edge to the other, leaving, of course, one edge row of mesh top and bottom on which the binding stitch is to be done later. Work through both layers of mesh on the fold-back as one, and do the same when you come to the thickness of three layers. Work right across your sewn-together edges, remember they are to be treated as one row of mesh.

A row of stitches spiralling around the canvas roll

When you start a row insert the needle diagonally in line with your path of stitches so that you will fasten down the beginning tag with its own color of wool. When you finish off a row run your thread back down in its own row of stitches as neatly as possible. Remember you won't be lining this case as the back of the stitches provide a finished enough appearance. Snip the wool tags off closely after working each thread. Work right around the canvas roll as if it were a whirling barber's pole. When the roll is completely covered with stripes and stitches, steam it flat with a hot iron and a damp cloth, and do any little stretching that is necessary. Let it dry. Then match up your mesh on one end, mesh for mesh on either side. Work the binding stitch over the two edges as if they were just one edge. Start with only one beginning stitch in the corner-most mesh. Then go ahead with the back and forth part of the stitch on the first set of matching mesh. Hide your wool ends in the body of the stitches. On the other end, the mouth of the case, work the binding stitch around the edge, running up on the two beginning stitches to make the stitch look as if it were continuous. Press once more to finish.

35

CHAPTER SIX

THE TRIVET

The trivet is made backwards, you "finish" it before you work the needlepoint. At least that is one way of doing it, the trivet can be done the conventional way if you prefer, that is, working the binding stitch last. The only advantage to "finishing" it first is that your work is a little more portable for carrying in your purse for that odd moment of work that you might snatch. It is more portable because the canvas size is reduced, no bare borders of canvas; and because the edges are tidier, the binding stitch has covered all little threads and sharp corners. The following instructions can be used for coasters too, so you could keep yourself going for some time on purse-size needlework by making a set of coasters, or a set of trivets.

The trivet may be worked on penelope or mono-canvas, but it is the most fun to work on rug canvas. Coasters will probably be more practical on finer mesh. Mark on the canvas the shape you want the trivet to be, six by six inches, five by seven, or three and one half by three and one half inches if you want to make a coaster. Count off the mesh, warp and woof, to see how many you have to work with in your design. The canvas pictured was worked in the Scotch stitch on rug canvas by a ten-year-old child. If you use the Scotch stitch too, your canvas must have mesh with a multiple of three.

The Trivet (needlepoint done by a ten-year-old child)

If you use mono-canvas don't forget to count two mesh for the actual fold of the canvas and then about five for the fold-back. Penelope and rug canvas need only one set of mesh for the fold, and four for the fold-back. Count these extra mesh out for all four sides and then cut your canvas.

Snip out very carefully a four mesh square from each corner

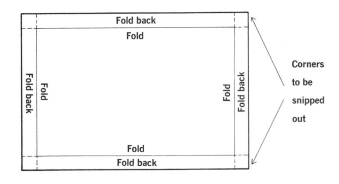

The Binding Stitch turning corner on a single thickness of canvas

of the canvas (five on mono-canvas). Fold the canvas back on the fifth row of mesh (six and seven on mono-canvas). Match up the three layers of mesh so that you can look through all three layers as if they were one. Baste the corner with carpet thread and with a few over and over stitches lash the raw edge of the canvas corner to the folded edge. Baste your way along the fold-back to the next corner and give it the same treatment. Continue around the canvas until all four corners are lashed and all fold-backs are basted down.

Work the binding stitch around the edge of the trivet. Work around the corners just the same as the straight-away. Treat the corner mesh hole just as you would any other hole, it receives no special treatment. Work over the beginning two stitches when you

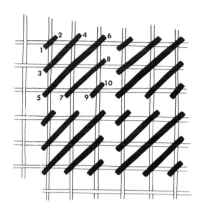

The Scotch Stitch

meet them again to give a continuous edge. You are now ready to
do the actual needlepoint.

When the work is completed, steam it with an iron and
damp cloth and pull it into shape again. It should not require a
complete blocking job. Trace the trivet's outline on a piece of
paper and then cut out the outline as a pattern for the felt bottom.
Steam any wrinkles out of the felt and then glue it to the bottom
of the trivet with a vinyl glue used sparingly or an artist's glue such
as rabbit skin. Pink the edges if you like. If you can lay your hands
on thin sheets of cork, it makes a fine bottom too.

CHAPTER SEVEN

THE BELT

The belt is made in just the same way as the trivet. It can be made of any canvas, remembering only to use one set of mesh for the fold on penelope canvas and two mesh if you use mono-canvas. The wool you use should be fairly fat for the job, a belt receives much friction on its edges and the corners will poke through unless the wool is adequate. If you do not plan to line the belt with ribbon, use a stitch that covers both sides of the canvas such as the basket-weave version of the half cross stitch or, as shown in the illustration, the mosaic stitch done diagonally. These instructions can also be used for a bell pull or luggage straps. Since you will probably want to line these any stitch will do.

Your waist measurement must be taken so that you will know how long the belt must be. Add a quarter of an inch at each

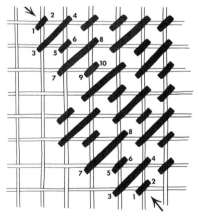

The Mosaic Stitch done diagonally

Showing the use of a stitch that covers the canvas on both sides

The lower side of the "v" is the underneath side.

41

end to cover any loss from stitch draw-up. An inch and a half is a good width for a belt. Count off your fold-back mesh, four or more depending on the fineness of the canvas. If you plan to use a symmetrical design make sure the working area mesh count is an even count. Cut your canvas.

Now you are ready to cut out the four mesh squares from the corners of the canvas as you did with the trivet. Match up the mesh three layers deep, and tack them in place with carpet thread, lashing the cut edge to the folded edge. Baste the two length-wise fold-backs down closely, this can be snipped out as you work the belt. The canvas has a tendency to ravel in the middle if this is not done. Work your design. Steam the belt with a damp cloth and a hot iron, and stretch and pull it back into shape again.

Start working the binding stitch from the middle of the belt along the fold. If the wool does not cover the corners tightly enough it may be necessary to work each side of the corner mesh. Work it from one side of the corner, then from the other side just as if it were a fresh mesh hole to work.

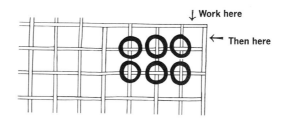

↓ Work here

← Then here

When you reach the beginning of the binding stitch again work over the first two stitches to give it a continuous look. Steam it again and then sew a pair of coat-size hooks and eyes in place at the ends. Any notions shop will carry these giant hooks and eyes.

42

CHAPTER EIGHT

THE EASY PINCUSHION

The easy pincushion is very quick to work up and simple to finish. It could conceivably be enlarged and designed as a pillow on rug canvas but otherwise penelope is really the canvas to use for this project. Tapestry wool or its equivalent would be the wool to use.

Mark off with a pencil on a piece of penelope canvas a rectangle six inches by three and one half inches. Allow a bare border of canvas an inch and one half wide on all four sides. Cut the canvas. Bind the edges all around with masking tape or binding tape to prevent raveling as you work the canvas.

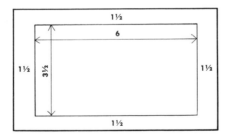

Make a simple design for your pincushion because it will be quite small when you have finished it and you won't have many mesh to work with. The cushion pictured here has two stripes of

the Bazar stitch and one broad stripe of Gobelin tramé. Directions for these stitches will be found on pages 46 and 47.

When you have worked the canvas, thread a needle with a six inch piece of carpet thread and run it in and out of the canvas through one straight line of stitches about an inch from one of the short ends of the canvas. This thread will be pulled out after finishing but its presence will help you greatly in lining up the ends of the cushion evenly.

In order to sew up the back seam (the short ends of the canvas), fold along the line of mesh next to the needlepoint. Do this on both sides of the canvas. Hold the folds together and, matching them mesh for mesh, baste them with an over and over stitch with carpet thread. Then thread your needle with the proper

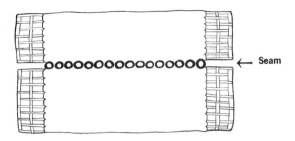

wool and stitch right up the row of basted mesh just as though it were a row of needlepoint you had missed. Use the half cross stitch.

Next trim the bare canvas to within four or five mesh of the seam. You will probably have to turn the canvas inside out to do this. Turn it right side out again and trim the canvas at each end of the cushion to within five or six mesh of the needlepoint. Turn in these five or six mesh at each end of the needlepoint roll you have produced, leaving just one row of mesh peeking over the worked area. Press these turn-ins in place with a damp cloth and hot iron. Press the seam you have completed, also. Using the carpet thread guide previously inserted, line up the top and bottom of the cushion so that they are true again and then press the whole thing flat.

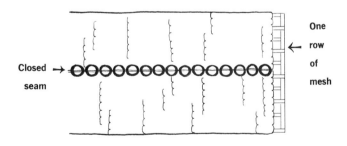

Border folded in and ready for the Binding Stitch

45

Work the binding stitch over both rows of mesh produced by folding the canvas border in. Work just one beginning stitch more as an anchor than a beginning. Work it over the corner-most mesh, it will also serve to help cover the corner canvas. Then go on with the back and forth part of the stitch on the first matching mesh. Match mesh for mesh as usual. Finish off the thread by running it through the body of stitches. Before working the binding stitch over the other end to close it, stuff the cushion with about half an ounce of lamb's wool, which may be obtained at any drug store. Work the binding stitch over the opening and the cushion is finished.

THE ''BAZAR'' STITCH

The October 2 1869 issue of *Harper's Bazar* (it was spelt with one A then) magazine included directions for the following stitch for which they had no name. It is more suitable as a specimen stitch than as a row stitch. It uses less wool than one

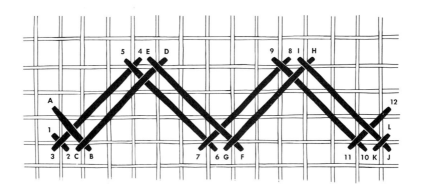

Work numbers first, then letters; proceed towards the right until you meet the number row.

The Bazar Stitch

would expect. This stitch can only be worked on two thread canvas as it slips down a mesh on mono-canvas. The diagram shows how to start the stitch and the photograph shows how it looks when completed. Six journeys across the canvas are required to complete the stitch. Weave in any missing stitches at the beginning and the end.

GOBELIN TRAMÉ

The May 1856 issue of *Peterson's Magazine* shows a stitch that Mrs. Stephens, one of the editors, calls mosaic tapestry. This is a misnomer, basically the stitch is a combination of tramé and the upright Gobelin stitch. *Peterson's Magazine* suggests doing the tramé in braid, gold or silver, or in straw.

47

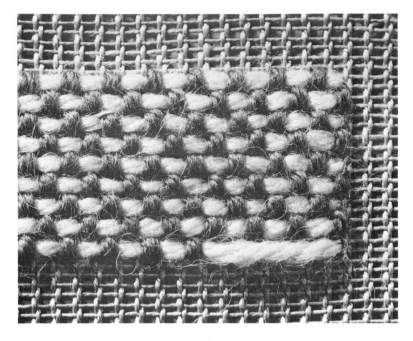

The Gobelin Tramé

The important thing to remember when selecting your wool for this stitch is that the tramé thread must completely cover the two threads of mesh over which the upright Gobelin will be done. Tapestry wool fits very well over ten mesh penelope and fourteen mesh mono-canvas. Persian wool using the full three thread strand will do on the fourteen mesh mono-canvas. It also works well on eighteen mesh mono-canvas when used single thread doubled over in the needle. Crewel wool will serve on the same canvas. This stitch should be experimented with to find the materials which best fit your canvas. The stitch loses its neat look on rug canvas because then two threads of wool must be used for the tramé to cover the mesh.

48

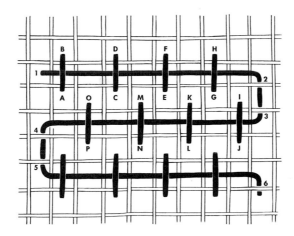

The Gobelin Tramé

The tramé in this stitch is laid on in a different manner than other tramé. It is laid over an entire row of mesh just before one works the upright Gobelin over that mesh row. It is done this way to keep from showing gaps in the tramé and to keep the tension loose enough. The stitch does not use as much wool as one would think.

49

CHAPTER NINE

THE PILLOW

The pillow can be made on any canvas using any matching wool, but this method of finishing a pillow lends itself proportionately to large canvas and wool. Fine mesh canvas seems to call for a more "important" edging than the binding stitch. If you really want to make a pillow using this method of finishing, why not try

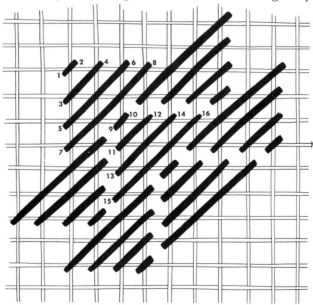

The Milanese Stitch

a fringe of wool all around the edge instead? Directions on how to make the fringe will be found on page 54.

The fancy stitches look quite smart on pillows, but if you plan to use one make sure you allow enough mesh to complete the stitch. For instance, with some stitches you need a multiple of three mesh, others six, some just two. The diagonally striped pillow in the illustration was done in the Milanese stitch. A pillow in this stitch works up very quickly.

The pillow is worked on one long piece of canvas. An empty row of mesh separates the two worked areas. Any number of mesh will do in each direction as far as size is concerned, just so the one half matches the other with the empty row in between for the fold. Your pillow could be large and square or small and oblong, a little neck pillow perhaps. If you use mono-canvas use two mesh threads for the fold. Allow four mesh for the fold-back (four sets of two threads) and one (set) for the fold if you use large two-thread canvas, and six or seven mesh for the fold-back if you use mono-canvas plus the aforementioned two threads of mesh for the actual fold.

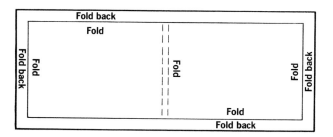

After you have cut the canvas, with your ever faithful carpet thread near by, snip a four mesh square out of each corner (or as many as your fold-back is for mono-canvas). Fold on the next row of mesh. Match up the mesh on the corner so that you can see through the three layers of canvas clearly. Baste the corner together and then lash the cut edge to the folded edge of the canvas with an over and over stitch. This will prevent the canvas from raveling as you work. Loosely baste the fold-back to the body of the canvas as you work from corner to corner. These threads may be pulled out as you work the needlepoint, if you wish.

Remember as you work the canvas to leave that center row of mesh bare. When you have finished working both halves of the canvas, you will probably have to give it the full blocking treatment to bring it back into shape. Wet it thoroughly and pull it gently back into shape. Tack it with aluminum tacks to a paper-covered board until dry. Try to use as few tacks as possible because you will be tacking by necessity right through your finished work, not bare canvas.

To make the cushion to go inside, run up three seams on an old piece of sheeting or curtain lining and then stuff it with kapok or foam rubber, which can be bought at the yard goods counter. Don't make the cushion until you have blocked your canvas because you will want to measure for it from the blocked canvas so that it will fit just right. After stuffing close the fourth seam.

When your canvas is dry, fold it along the unworked row (or rows) of mesh and proceed to do the binding stitch along the row thus prepared.

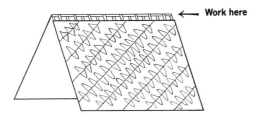

When you reach the corner of the canvas work right around it just as though it were the straight-away. Then match mesh for mesh as you work down the two edges of the canvas, binding them together. When you have done the fold and two sides, insert the cushion and close up the last side. Turn the last corner and work into the first two beginning stitches. If a little canvas shows in the corners, don't worry, you can oversew the corners a few stitches or loop a tassel through each corner or work each side of the corner mesh as described in the directions for the belt. Steam press the edges just a little to give them a flatter look.

53

Showing fringe, one loop needs to be pulled tight

FRINGE EDGING

After the canvas is blocked whip the edges together with carpet thread, matching mesh for mesh. (Of course, insert the pillow first.) To make the fringe, cut your wool in six inch pieces and with a crochet hook, draw the wool through the edge mesh, catching it with the hook right in the middle. (See Figure 1.) Then put the hook through the loop you just made, draw the ends that

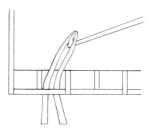

Figure 1

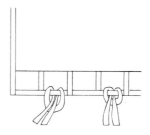

Figure 2

are sticking out on the other side through the loop and tighten. (See Figure 2.) It might be well to put more than one loop of fringe through the meshes at the corners, as many as three or four. When the fringe is attached all around the pillow, trim it to the desired length, using a cardboard gauge so that you can barber it evenly.

Another rug canvas pillow, worked in Half Cross Stitch

CHAPTER TEN

THE ENVELOPE PURSE

The envelope purse can be made on rug canvas or smaller mesh canvas but is more fun and easier to make on rug canvas. It could be made as part of a set, that is, the envelope purse for inside a tote bag. One could take part of the design of the tote bag and repeat it on the flap of the envelope purse. A lingerie case could be made of pale colors, or a brief case of strong bright ones.

To design the purse make a paper pattern of the size you want it to be, say seven inches wide by fourteen inches long. The width should be half the length for planning purposes. Fold the pattern into the shape of the purse, leaving about three inches for the front top flap. Draw pencil lines at the folds. If you plan to

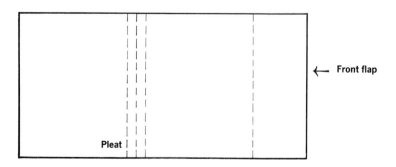

56

An Envelope Purse (needlepoint done by a nine-year-old child)

have a pleated bottom on the purse (see page 59) fold about an inch and a half of the paper pattern up into a pleat on the bottom fold. Draw lines on the pleat folds. Lay your paper pattern on your canvas, trace around its outline and mark where the folds and pleat folds will come. Count the mesh enclosed by the outline. Now you can design your purse knowing just about how much space you have for the front, back and flap.

Having planned your design, allow for the usual five mesh

for the fold and fold-back around all four sides of the traced out-line on the canvas. (Six or seven mesh for the finer mesh canvas.) Cut your canvas and snip out a four mesh square from each corner of the canvas. (If you are using finer mesh canvas you will cut out five or six mesh squares.) You must figure on two threads of mesh for the fold if you use mono-canvas.

Fold the fold-backs and match up the mesh in each corner so that you can see through all three layers, square for square. With your carpet thread tack the corners and then with an over and over stitch lash the raw edge to the folded edge to prevent later raveling. Baste the fold-back to the body of the canvas all the way around. Work your design on the canvas.

Steam the purse when you have finished the needlepoint if it is only slightly stretched out of shape. If it is badly lop-sided,

Lining stitched into place, exposing only canvas on which binding stitch will be worked

wet it, stretch it true, and tack it to a paper-covered board with aluminum tacks. Use the tacks sparingly as you will be tacking through finished work. When the canvas is dry, cut out a piece of lining material just a third of an inch larger all the way around than the purse. Turn in the raw edge and neatly blind stitch the lining into place, leaving exposed the fold of mesh on which you will do the binding stitch.

If you used the seven by fourteen inch dimensions for the purse you must now measure four inches from the end opposite the flap and fold the canvas. If you used your own dimensions fold at the appropriate place for the pleat. Measure another inch and a half and fold again. Pinch the folds together to make the pleat and hold in place with straight pins. Make sure each half of the pleat has an equal number of mesh exposed on the edge. For instance, if you have four mesh on each pleat side, you will have eight mesh facing you on the bottom of the pleat.

Work the binding stitch across these stitches, starting on the left end and working to the end on the right. Dispense with the beginning stitches, start with the back and forth part of the stitch right away. Treat the other side of the purse in the same way, folding across the canvas on one line of mesh to make sure your

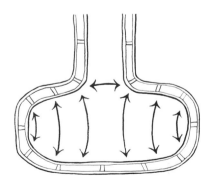

pleats are evenly placed. Starting from the pleat, work the binding stitch all the way around the purse from pleat to pleat. Dispense with the beginning two stitches altogether and start right out with the back and forth part, working through the two thicknesses matching mesh for mesh, on up the flap and then down to the two thicknesses again. Work your wool into the pleat stitches at both ends so that it is not obvious just where the stitch starts and ends. Work the binding stitch (without the beginning stitches) across

The pleat being worked

the remaining edge at the mouth of the purse. Sew a very large snap to the inside of the flap and to the front of the purse. Steam iron the pleats and folds into place.

If you don't wish to have a pleated purse, fold the purse about five inches from the end opposite to the flap and work the binding stitch from double thicknesses to single edge and back to double thicknesses.

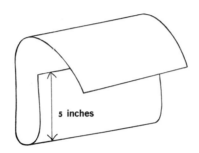

5 inches

61

The Side Panel Tote (the other side repeats only the crab motif)

CHAPTER ELEVEN

THE SIDE PANEL TOTE

To make this tote of anything but rug canvas *is* humanly possible, but is not really advisable unless you are heavily endowed with eyesight and patience. To match up the mesh of the side panels and the body of the canvas on anything smaller than five mesh canvas would be very tedious and fraught with possibilities for mistakes and frustration. Rug wool or a suitable bulky knitting wool are the recommended wools. The tote can be lined in cotton, or in plastic if you plan to use it for the beach or for baby paraphernalia.

The main part of the tote is made in one long piece, as many mesh long as you wish. You must plan for mesh for the bottom and the same number of mesh for both front and back.

Two side panels must be made, measuring the same height as the front (and back) and as many mesh wide on the bottom as you have for the bottom of the main piece. This can be shown in a formula for better understanding:

tote side + bottom + tote side
$$= \text{panel side} + \text{bottom} + \text{panel side}$$

The panel sides will be attached to the main part of the tote with the binding stitch.

63

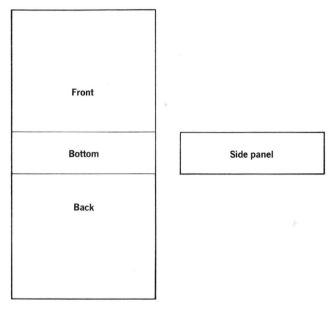

First count out the mesh for the main piece of canvas. The tote illustrated was made on five mesh rug canvas and is fifty-two mesh wide; the front and back measure forty-two mesh with eight mesh for the bottom, a total of ninety-two mesh. Five mesh or more were added at each end for finishing, and five mesh were added to each side for the fold-back and the fold.

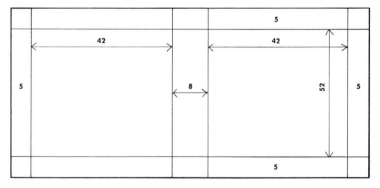

Fold the canvas along the long sides on the fifth mesh in. Baste it to the body of the canvas with carpet thread. Cover the short ends of the canvas with masking tape to prevent raveling. You now have a forty-two by fifty-two mesh space for your design. If you plan to use a fancy stitch try to choose one which will not pull the canvas too much out of shape. Blocking will bring it back into shape but constant use of the tote might cause it to slip back into its crooked ways. If you design a motif for the tote instead, select part of it and repeat it on the back to make that part of the tote less boring to work. Work the main part of your tote, working right through the fold-backs as usual.

The side panels must be the exact number of mesh as the main piece sides, thus with a forty-two mesh front and back and an eight mesh bottom, your side panel will have forty-two mesh on the long sides, and eight mesh on the bottom. Add five mesh on all sides, at the top for later finishing and on the sides and bottom for the fold-back and fold.

Snip a four mesh square out of the bottom corners of each side panel. Fold the long sides back on the fifth mesh in, and then fold the bottom up. With carpet thread baste the corners so the three layers of mesh match exactly square on square. With an over

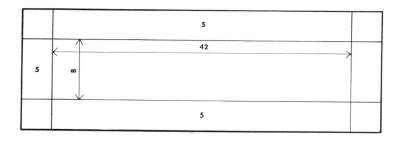

and over stitch lash down the cut edge to the folded edge of the canvas to prevent raveling. Baste the fold-back to the body of the canvas. Cover the raw edge at the top with masking tape. You are now ready to work the side panels. They may be worked in plain half cross stitch or in the fancy stitch of your choice. If you work them too tightly, they will curl. Work through both layers of mesh right to the fold and through all three layers at the corners.

When the side panels are finished they should be steamed into shape with a wet cloth and hot iron. If they really need a good blocking, tack through the work at the bottom and through the excess canvas at the top. Block the main piece if necessary by tacking through the excess canvas at the top and bottom.

When all three pieces are completed, you are ready to binding stitch them together. Start at the first row of completed work on each piece. Holding the side panel and the main piece together, wrong sides facing each other, work the binding stitch mesh for mesh down the front of the bag, treating the double row of mesh as if it were just one. When you come to the bottom of the front (and the side panel) fold the main piece so that its mesh will match the bottom of the side panel. Stitch right around the corner as though you were still on the straight-away. Be careful to work on the outside of the stitches completed, don't thrust your needle into the body of completed binding stitches.

If you have any doubts that this process will work, baste the side panels onto the main piece first, mesh for mesh, and then you will be sure they will come out even in the end. When both sides are in, fold the excess canvas at the top down into the tote, leaving one row of mesh exposed on which to work a row of binding stitch as an edging. Work the binding stitch around the row thus created in one continuous chain from panel to panel, working over the

Completed side panel

Large piece being wrapped around side panel by the Binding Stitch, one corner completed

first two beginning stitches as usual. Trim the excess canvas to within three mesh of the edging and securely baste it to the back of the work.

Folded canvas for handle, with Binding Stitch worked on one half

To make the handles, cut two strips of canvas fourteen inches long by eight mesh wide. Count in three mesh on the long side and fold on that third mesh. Do the same on the other side. You now should have a strip four mesh wide if you count the folded mesh.

Work the binding stitch *over* the depth of two mesh the length of the strip. Start one inch along the strip and finish one inch short. So that the handle may have a braided look you must work the other side starting at the same end you did on the first side. Make another handle just like the first. When they are completed, stitch them into place with carpet thread. Stitch through that bare inch of canvas at each end. The worked part of the handle should not extend down below the row of binding stitch at the top of the tote. Be sure to attach the handles securely.

Cut and stitch the lining, using the inside measurements of the bag as a guide. Pin the lining into place. Remember that the selvedge at the top cuts down on bulk. Blind stitch the lining right under the binding stitch edging. Block the corners and folds with a damp cloth and hot iron to give the bag a finished look.

A pocket can be added to the outside of the bag. With the top edge of the pocket folded back, tack it to the tote after first working the area that would be covered by it. Then work right through the two layers of canvas, over the pocket's single thickness, and then through the two layers again. Finish the top folded edge with the Binding Stitch and a button and loop.

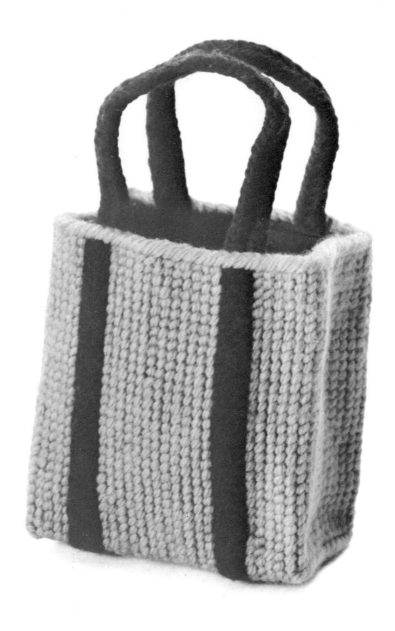

The One-Piece Tote (needlepoint done by the same child who did the trivet, page 37)

CHAPTER TWELVE

THE ONE-PIECE TOTE

The one-piece tote is really best suited to rug canvas if "quick and easy" is your first consideration. Ten mesh penelope or mono-canvas will work as well if you don't mind working on a piece of canvas as big as a piano bench cover, and if you have plenty of time to work on it. You need not conform to the square-shaped tote, this one may be designed as a shoe carrier. To figure the canvas needed for a shoe carrier, measure one of your shoes, double that amount, add two inches plus three for the bottom. The width should be about ten inches from seam to seam.

The main thing to remember in designing is that you must have an uneven number of mesh lengthwise. That little uneven mesh will be the key to joining the two sides later. Otherwise, any number of mesh will do in either direction. Decide on the shape you want and count off the mesh. Count off an extra five mesh on the two long sides for the fold and the fold-back. (Allow more if you use mono-canvas, plus two mesh for the fold.) The short ends should have an inch and a half of excess canvas allowed. Cut your canvas. Fold the long sides on the fifth mesh in, and baste them down. Cover the unfolded ends with masking tape so that they will not ravel as you work. Fold the canvas in half to find the middle mesh, that uneven one mentioned above.

On the folded edge of the canvas mark the exact middle

71

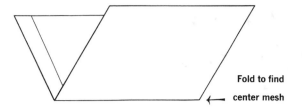

Fold to find
center mesh

mesh. Do this on both sides. From that center mark count off in both directions half the number of mesh wide you want the side of the tote to be. Then, from the folded edge, count the same number of mesh in, plus one. For instance, if you want a fifteen mesh wide side, count off seven mesh up the canvas *from* the middle mesh and then seven mesh down from the middle mesh. Mark again with pencil. *Including* the fold mesh, count eight mesh into the center of the canvas and draw a line parallel to the side.

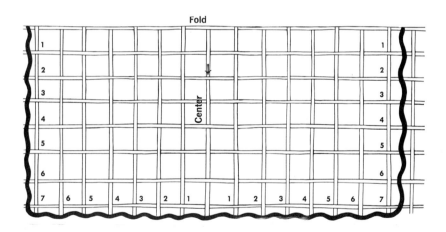

Mark off the other side of the canvas in the same way. These areas will not be worked, they will be your boxed corners later. Now that you have your limits, you may design your bag, remembering that the bottom will be fifteen mesh wide (or whatever number you have chosn) and the sides seven mesh wide plus the fold.

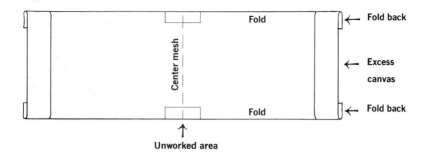

As you work the tote, stitch right through the fold-back as usual. The tote illustrated on page 70 has two fern stitch stripes. The stripes were worked in the opposite direction from each other so that they would look like one continuous loop when connected with the handles.

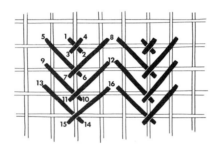

The Fern Stitch

When the work is finished, the canvas will have to be either steam-pressed or blocked, depending on how badly it is stretched out of shape. If it needs blocking, wet it thoroughly, pull it true again and then tack it with aluminum tacks to a paper-covered board. Tack it through the excess canvas at the top and bottom as much as possible.

After you have removed your dry canvas from the board, snip a rectangle of canvas from that unworked area about four mesh in and about nine mesh wide.

73

Canvas worked except for cut-out area, piece already cut out

Snip a piece the same size from the other unworked area. Now leave these areas for the moment and match up the sides of the tote back to front, mesh for mesh. With your trusty carpet thread stitch the sides together through the fold mesh so that they themselves form a row of mesh up the side of the tote. Start with the first worked row on each side. With your background color wool work a row of half cross stitch up the row, thus making sort of a hidden seam. Treat the other side the same way, basting the mesh first, then over-stitching with wool.

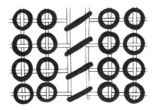

Mesh basted with carpet thread

Return to the unworked area, tuck all the unworked canvas inside the bag except for one row of mesh all around. You will be "closing the mouth" of mesh with the binding stitch but first baste it with carpet thread as a reinforcement. Holding the "mouth" closed and matching mesh for mesh, start basting at the corner. When it is basted together work the binding stitch over the closed

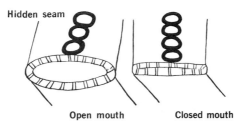

Hidden seam

Open mouth   Closed mouth

Mouth closing, the Binding Stitch being worked

mouth. Work your beginning stitches in that corner mesh, using the first set of matched mesh for the actual first binding stitch. If any bare canvas shows in the corners when you are finished, bluff in a few covering stitches now. Work the other "mouth" the same way. Using a damp cloth and a hot iron, steam the edges of the tote to give it the proper shape.

To finish the top, fold down the excess canvas leaving one row of mesh exposed on which to work the binding stitch. Work the binding stitch around the mesh after you have basted the excess canvas to the body of the tote.

You will need two strips of canvas eight mesh wide and as long as you like to make the handles. Twelve or fourteen inches make a good-sized handle. Count in three mesh on the long side and fold the length of the canvas. Count in three mesh on the other side of the canvas and fold. You now have a handle four mesh wide. Starting to work an inch from the end, work the binding stitch over the edge of the canvas a depth of two mesh, finishing an inch short of the end.

Starting from the same end as before, work the binding stitch down the other side. Work the second handle the same way and attach them securely with your carpet thread to the body of the tote, working through that bare inch of canvas at the end of each handle. The worked part of the handle should not extend down below the row of binding stitch at the top of the tote.

Measure the inside of the tote for the dimensions of the lining. Using the selvedge of the material at the mouth of the tote cuts down on bulk. The lining should be made in the same general pattern as the tote to insure a good fit, i.e. two side seams and boxed corners. Blind stitch the lining into place right under the row of binding stitch at the top of the bag. Steam press the whole thing to smarten up its appearance.

CHAPTER THIRTEEN

THE TWO-PIECE PINCUSHION

The two-piece pincushion is not for the novice needle-pointer or for the novice binding stitcher. Previous experience is required to do this project justice. It is not that the designing is hard or that the working of the needlepoint is intricate, it is just that the joining of the pieces takes patience and some engineering skill.

Any canvas will do for this project, mono-canvas or penelope. If you want to make a small pillow using this pattern, rug canvas will do. Fourteen mesh per inch mono-canvas or ten mesh per inch penelope will work very well. Three inches by three inches by an inch and a half are good dimensions for a pincushion of this sort. The top piece of canvas will look like a cross in design, with a square of bare canvas in each corner. It could be designed as a rectangle if you wish. The important thing to remember in designing it is that the gusset mesh must match exactly on each side and the sides of the bottom piece must match exactly the sides of the top piece, mesh for mesh.

The construction of the pincushion is quite simple. The top piece is just a piece of canvas with the four corners nipped in. The bottom piece is flat, fitting or matching the top piece precisely. To prepare the canvas for working, outline the cross of the

top piece in pencil, counting out the mesh to make sure the sides are even. Add five mesh on each end of the arms of the cross for the fold and fold-back, six mesh if you use mono-canvas. (Don't forget to use two threads of mesh for the actual folds on mono-canvas.) Cut the canvas. Fold back the four sides of the arms four mesh, folding on the fifth mesh in. (For mono-canvas, fold back four mesh also.) Tack the corners of the canvas with carpet thread just to keep them from raveling as you work, it is not necessary to do any mesh matching on the corners this time because you will not be needlepointing in that area of the canvas. The corners of the canvas will be cut out when you are finishing the pincushion.

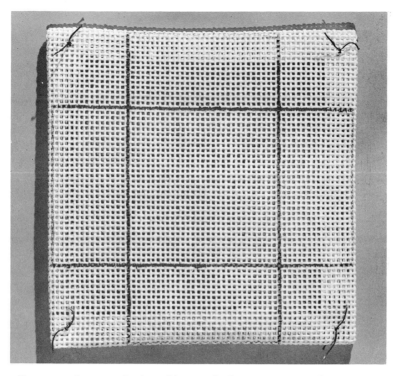

Canvas ready to work pincushion, tacked corners to be left unworked

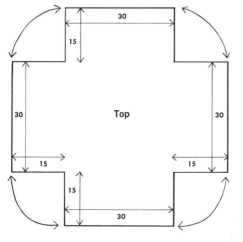

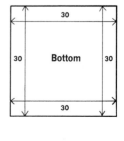

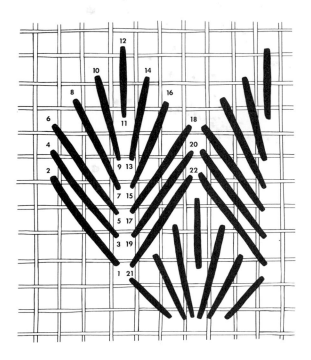

The Leaf Stitch

Tuck a half cross stitch in the apex of each of the four corners. Doing this will make a neater corner on the cushion when completed. The pincushion pictured was worked in the leaf stitch and the half cross stitch worked in four directions to form a rough star shape. If you plan to use a fancy stitch be sure to count out the multiple of the stitch correctly so that you won't split a stitch awkwardly. Stitch right through the fold-backs as you have on previous projects, as though working on just one thickness of canvas.

The bottom piece must have all four sides folded back, a four mesh square having been first snipped out from each corner. Match up the three layers of mesh as usual when you fold the canvas, mesh on top of mesh. Lash the cut edge to the folded edge so that the cut edge will not ravel as you work. Since the bottom of

80

the pincushion will not show it is not necessary to design for it. Here is a good place, however, to put your initials and the date. Work the fold-back and the corners as though they were one layer of canvas, leaving only the folded edge free of stitches.

When you have completed both pieces they should be steamed with a damp cloth and a hot iron. Since the pieces are so small they should not require more than a good steaming to make them true again.

The corners of the top must be gusseted first, so fold the corners in. Start the binding stitch at the inside corner, using the first holes that present themselves. Dispense with the beginning two stitches of the binding stitch, start right out with the back and forth part. Use two threads of mesh if you are working on mono-canvas on each side of the gusset or one set of mesh on each side if penelope. You will find that if very coarse mono-canvas such as ten mesh is used you will have to use just one thread of mesh on each side, otherwise the binding stitch does not cover the canvas. Keep checking as you work to make sure you are matching mesh for mesh on each side; you don't want to come out uneven. If by chance you should make a mistake, snip out the whole offending seam and start over again.

Try to hold the work the way the pieces will be when finished. When you are about two-thirds down the seam trim the excess canvas from the corner to within five mesh of the needle-point. Snip up into the corner within three mesh. Finish the gusset to the last set of mesh and work the other three gussets in like fashion.

Though you have planned for the top and bottom to be square, the tension of the stitches will have made two sides slightly longer than the other two. Therefore you must match the upper piece long sides with the bottom piece long sides when you join

The gusset closing. Canvas used in photo sample was ten mesh mono-canvas, too heavy to pick up two threads of mesh on each side.

top and bottom. This lengthening does not always happen, it depends on the tightness of your stitches and the stitch you used.

Starting from any corner, hold the top and bottom together and work the binding stitch over the two edges, making them one. Treat the corners as though they were the straight-away. If you match mesh for mesh, top and bottom, you should have no trouble. As you reach the corners of the bottom piece where carpet thread was used to lash the cut edge, you must now snip out the lashing threads carefully just before you work the corner.

Stuff the pincushion before you bind up the fourth side. A three by three inch cushion should take about one ounce of lambs wool, which can be purchased at any drug store. Stuff the cushion fairly full and then bind up the last side. Work into your beginning stitches just one or two stitches when you met them again. With a damp cloth and a hot iron smarten up the corners a bit.

If you made a small cushion, the finishing instructions are the same except that a pillow of any scrap material should be made in the same dimensions as the needlepoint. It should be stuffed with kapok or foam rubber and inserted in the needlepoint cover after you have binding stitched two sides of the top and bottom.

CHAPTER FOURTEEN

THE TYPEWRITER COVER

For this project rug canvas and bulky knitting wool or rug wool is recommended. The typewriter cover pictured was made for an electric office machine, which has a deeper chassis than a manual office machine. If your machine is a manual, shorten the three pieces of the cover one inch from front to back. The directions will be given by inches for the electric machine.

The main piece of canvas must measure seventeen inches wide to cover the carriage and the carriage return lever. It must measure thirty-three inches long, nine inches for the back, twelve inches for the top and twelve inches for the keys. If your design is representational it should center on the front twenty-three inches.

The two side panels must measure seventeen and a half inches along the bottom, eight and three-quarters inches high; the top should measure eleven and three-quarters inches and the lower front should measure four and one-half inches. A forty-five degree angle, which will take care of the rest of the front, will measure eight and one quarter inches. Make a paper pattern of the side panels first before you try to figure it out on the canvas. Save the pattern as you will use it later when making the lining of the cover.

The cover pictured has the mosaic stitch done as a frame to the motto, the side panels and background are done in half cross stitch. Not all fancy stitches are suitable for this project because that forty-five degree angle necessitates cutting stitches right down the middle.

Work the main piece first. Allow five mesh for the fold-back and the fold on three sides of the canvas, i.e., the long sides and the front. Allow a few extra mesh leeway on the back end of the main piece, you may need them as a result of using more in the finishing than expected. Then allow an inch and a half bare canvas border. Count in five mesh and fold on that mesh on the three aforemen-

tioned sides. Clip four mesh out of the two front corners. Match up the three layers of mesh, square for square in those corners and with your carpet thread lash the cut edge to the folded edge to prevent raveling. Baste the fold-back to the body of the canvas

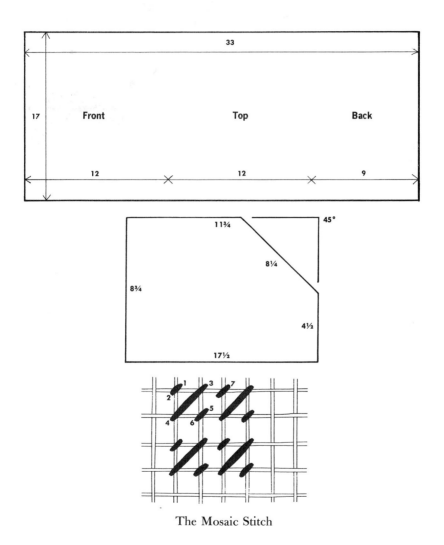

The Mosaic Stitch

along the front and the two long sides. Put some masking tape or binding tape on the raw canvas edge of the back to prevent raveling. You are now ready to work the canvas, starting from front to back.

To cut the canvas for your side panels, lay the paper pattern on *two* layers of canvas and pin it in place. Pencil a line around the pattern and remove it. Draw another line around the first outline about five mesh out. On the forty-five degree side the line should be an inch and a half away from the first line. Cut the canvas on the second line.

Fold the canvas along the first pencilled line on the bottom and the back. On the back bottom corner snip out the four mesh square, match up the three layers of canvas and baste with the carpet thread as usual, lashing the cut edge to the folded edge. Baste the fold-back to the body of the canvas on the bottom and the back. The top, the forty-five degree angle, and the little front section should be left flat. They may be covered with masking tape. When you fold the edges back on the other side panel, make sure they are not folded in the same direction as on the first side.

When all three pieces are worked, block the main piece carefully, making sure its sides are straight and true. The side pieces probably won't require more than a damp cloth and a hot iron plus a tug or two to straighten them.

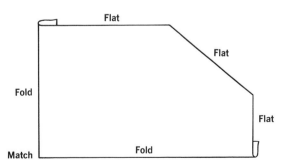

To join the main part of the cover to the side panels you must start working from the front and work to the back. Starting at the first row of stitches on each piece, and holding the main piece and the side panel with their wrong sides together, work the binding stitch up the short straight front. Match mesh for mesh while stitching through the two mesh as if they were one. When you come to the angle you must start handling the binding stitch in a new way. On one side of the canvas (the main piece) you will thrust the needle in the customary hole, on the other side, (the angled side panel) the needle will go into the peak of the mesh for two stitches and then into the side of the peak of the mesh for one stitch. You must go literally into the side of the peak, that means between the two threads of the mesh. This is not necessary when you are working the peak stitches. The sides of the peaks are used because otherwise there just wouldn't be enough mesh to match up with the main piece. Always use the right side of the peak, not the left, it will give you a better shaped line.

As you work up the forty-five degree angle count the mesh on the main piece so that you will know how many you are using.

Joining the straight main piece to the forty-five degree angle side piece, the needle emerges from peaked mesh.

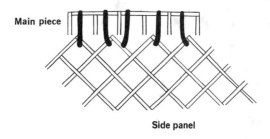

Main piece

Side panel

How to match up the mesh

The other side of the cover must use up the same number of mesh. This may sound like superfluous advice, but the cover will not work out evenly by mesh at the back if you use up too many mesh on the angle on one side. Work the straight-away at the top and around the corner and down the back. If you are a few rows short of needlepoint on the main piece or a few rows too many, just add the needed rows or pick out the extra rows. Binding stitch the other side panel to the main piece.

Baste the excess canvas on the back of the main piece to the finished underside, leaving one row of mesh exposed on which to work the binding stitch. Starting from the back of the cover work the binding stitch all the way around the edge. Overlap the first two beginning stitches to make the stitch look continuous. With a damp cloth and a hot iron steam the seams and corners into shape. Clip up into the angled corner to within two mesh of the seam, otherwise it is not really necessary to trim excess canvas.

Using your original paper pattern of the side panel cut out two pieces of your lining material. Remembering the measurements of the main piece cut out a lining for it. Stitch the linings together, clip close along the angle seam and into the corners. Blind stitch the lining into place right next to the binding stitch along the bottom. With cotton thread of matching color tack here and there through the needlework and the lining to keep the lining in place.

CHAPTER FIFTEEN

THE HUMPTY DUMPTY DOLL

The Humpty Dumpty doll is a rug canvas project using bulky knitting wool or rug wool. Infinite patience would be required to put him together using a finer canvas, even the King's men would have trouble. Preparing the canvas is relatively simple. Just count off the cross-shaped form of his body as shown in the diagram. Leave a border of unworked canvas around all the edges about six mesh deep. Cut the canvas and bind the edges with masking tape or binding tape to prevent raveling.

Follow the design on the diagram or make your own design, Humpty can be made without the surrey stitch hair if you prefer. The eyes were bordered with one split of the two-ply bulky wool used for the hair. The stitches were inserted between the half cross stitches with an over and over stitch. Work your canvas and when finished it should only require a good steaming with a damp cloth and a hot iron plus a few tugs here and there to make it true again.

Cut two strips of canvas eight mesh wide and seven inches long. It is important that the selvedge of the canvas be used at one narrow end of each strip. Cut two more strips eight mesh wide and nine or ten inches long, again using the selvedge at one end of each strip. The short strips will be Humpty's arms and the long strips his legs. They are prepared for working the same way you

prepared the tote handles on page 68, fold them on the third mesh in on both long sides.

You are now ready to start to put Humpty together. You will be working the binding stitch on the row of mesh closest to the needlework. Fold the bare canvas, leaving just this row of mesh

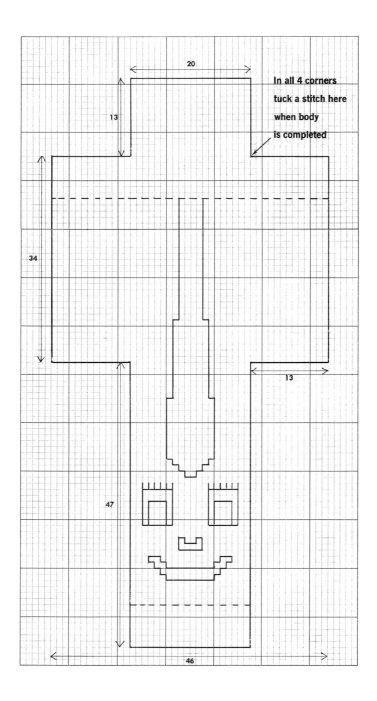

20

In all 4 corners
tuck a stitch here
when body
is completed

13

34

13

47

46

91

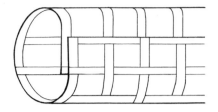

exposed. Humpty is put together somewhat like the two-piece pincushion, the four corners are gusseted. The canvas is tucked in and the binding stitch is worked over the edges thus presented. Dispense with the first two beginning stitches and start the binding stitch with the back and forth part at the top back of the head. Use the same color wool as the head and start on the first two mesh that present themselves. When you come to the corner work right around it, mesh for mesh, being careful not to put the needle into already worked stitches. Trim the bare canvas to within four mesh of the needlework as you work.

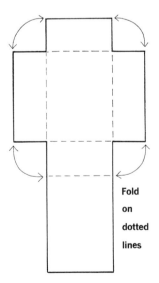

Fold
on
dotted
lines

Work the binding stitch on down his front to within two inches of the doll's pants. Insert the raw canvas end of one arm into the seam and calmly turn the corner from the body onto the arm. The arm should be about an inch deep into the body. Be careful as you turn the corner to use each hole that is presented, thus you will work the fold hole, then the middle hole and then up the middle holes as you did the tote handles. Work the binding stitch right up to the very end of the arm and then finish off the thread. To work the other side of Humpty's arm, start at the top of his pants, double checking the mesh to make sure they are even. You will be working from his pants top up to his arm pit, so to

Showing the arm inserted in the body and the Binding Stitch being worked around the corner in preparation to going up the arm

speak. Again calmly turn the corner, using each hole as it comes, and proceed up the arm. Work to the very end and then do five or six over and over stitches over the selvedge end, covering any little corners of canvas that might be peeking through.

Work the other side of the upper body and arm the same way. Using the pants color work the binding stitch down the front of Humpty's pants on each side. Omit the beginning stitches, start right off with the back and forth part of the binding stitch. Trim the canvas for the bottom half of Humpty. Join the gusset sides as you did on his head. Work around the corner and just one third of an inch along the front. Insert the raw canvas end of one of the legs into the seam about an inch. Turn the corner as you did on the arms and work to the end of the leg.

Leaving that leg for the moment, work the gusset on the other hip of the doll, turn the corner and stop. You will need half a pound or more of kapok to stuff Humpty and you must do it now before you insert the other leg. Work the kapok up into the corners with a ruler or pencil, stuff him fairly tight. Then you may insert the other leg, checking first to make sure the legs are even in length. Start working the binding stitch again from where you left it after turning the hip corner, insert the other leg and work its length. Now you have the insides of his legs left to do and a short stretch of bare mesh on the body. Starting from the middle of that bare stretch (skipping the beginning stitches again) work the binding stitch over to the leg and down it, finishing the leg off the way you did the arms with an over and over stitch. Work the inside of the other leg in the same fashion. Smarten up the corners of the body with a hot iron and a damp cloth. If you gave Humpty hair now is the time to trim it.

THE SURREY STITCH

This stitch is started at the bottom of the canvas and worked up. Ordinarily one would trim the pile as one worked but for the Humpty doll it is easier to trim after the doll is put together.

To start the stitch bring the needle in and out of the canvas as in diagram a. Holding down with your thumb the tag of wool left out, bring the needle and wool around to the left and insert it from the right in the space next door as in diagrams b and c. The needle must pass over its own tail, so to speak, to form the knot. Pull the wool tight and the knot is secure. To start the next stitch insert the needle at X as in diagram d. To start the next row begin on the row just above the row completed.

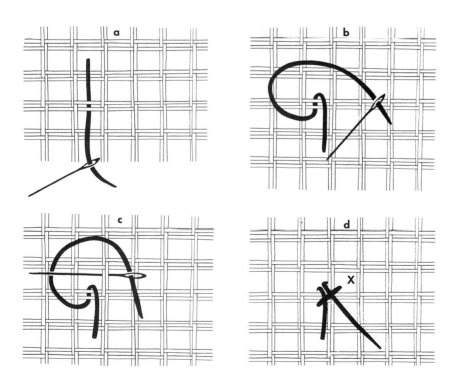

95

IN CONCLUSION

It is hoped that the making of these projects has brought to the reader some enjoyment plus an enlargement of her needlepoint horizon, particularly those readers who live in cities which do not have design needlepoint shops and who must depend on their own resources for project inspiration. Perhaps these projects will also enlarge the needlepoint scope of occupational therapists and craft teachers.

The reader, no doubt, will have thought of many variations to the projects given. Here are some more possibilities: a tea cosy using the forty-five degree angle binding from the typewriter cover; a long flapped glasses case using the envelope purse pattern; a cosmetic case with a zipper using the envelope purse pattern without a flap; a yardstick sheath; and finally, bedroom scuffs using a short forty-five degree angle for shape and then glued to rubber zori with the straps cut off.

The basic techniques are in this book, just let your imagination go wild, try anything, it might work!

BIBLIOGRAPHY

Aiguillette, Mrs. Pullan, *The Ladies' Manual of Fancy Works: A Complete Instructor In Every Variety of Ornamental Needlework,* New York, Dick and FitzGerald, 1859.

Harper's Bazar, Harper and Brothers, New York, October 2, 1869

Horne, Patience, (editor) *Stitched Rugs and Tapestries,* Brentford, Middlesex, England, Stitchcraft, Ltd.

Lewis, Griselda, (editor) *Handbook of Crafts,* London, E. Hulton & Co., Ltd., 1960

Peterson's Magazine, edited by Stephens, Mrs. Ann S., and Peterson, Charles J., Philadelphia, Pa., May 1856

Encyclopedia of Needlework, Hearthside Press, New York, 1965